MW01138033

Dick Powell

A One-Person Play
in Two Acts

By

Michael B. Druxman

The Hollywood Legends

Songs

"*When Irish Eyes Are Smiling*" written by Chauncey Olcott and George Graff, Jr.

"*The Ballad of Casey Jones*" Composer : Eddie Newton
Lyricists: Wallace Saunders, T. Lawrence Seibert

"*Over There*" Written by George M. Cohan.

"*Pretty Baby*" Words by Gus Kahn; Music by Tony Jackson and Egbert Van Alstyne.

TIME

Act I is set in 1944 in the home of Dick Powell and Joan Blondell.

Act II is set in 1956 in the home of Dick Powell and June Allyson.

SETTING

The home offices of Dick Powell.

The main entry to the home is O.S., UL; also access to the rest of the house.

Stylish furnishings include a desk with typewriter, armchair, coffee and end tables. Also in the room are a television set, a coffee-maker and a wet bar.

A framed photo of Joan Blondell sits on the desk.

Drapes cover sliding glass doors DR, which open to a swimming pool and the rest of the estate.

For Act II, the deor and furnishings will be updated, but their placement will remain, essentially, the same.

A famed photo of June Allyson will sit on the desk.

DICK POWELL

ACT I

>AT RISE: *The stage is empty.*
>O.S. *we hear* DICK POWELL, *singing*
>*"When Irish Eyes Are Smiling".*

POWELL (*O.S.*)
(*Sings*)
"When Irish Eyes are Smiling sure it's like a morn in spring.
"In the lilt of Irish laughter you can hear the angels sing...."

>*Powell, 40, enters* SL. *He wears a sport coat, slacks, white shirt; no tie.*

>*Spotting the audience, he stops singing.*

POWELL
(*Slightly surprised; friendly; To audience:*)
Hello.
(*Checks watch.*)
You're early.

That's okay. Have a seat. I just have a call or two to make.

You want some coffee?

He crosses to the desk. Peruses his personal address/phone book.

Don't get the wrong idea.

I'm not going to sing for you today.

I just do that around the house when I'm alone.
(Picks up phone; dials:)
I'm not even Irish. "Powell" is Welsh origin.
(Into phone:)
Hello. This is Dick Powell. Is he in?
(To audience:)
My agent.
(Into phone:)
Hi! Did you hear from Wilder yet?

Call him. Tell him we have another offer.

I know I don't have another offer...but he doesn't know that.
(Winks at audience.)
I want that part.

Okay, I'll be here. Call me back.
(Hangs up; Speaks to audience:)
I'm up for a Billy Wilder picture...with Barbara Stanwyck.

Double Indemnity.

No singing.

I'd play a murderer.

George Raft turned down the part.

He didn't want to play another bad guy.

I'd love to play a bad guy.

That would sure change my public image.
                    (*Dials phone.*)
One more, then I'm all yours...until the phone rings.
                    (*Into phone:*)
Operator, get me the Plaza Hotel in New York.
                    (*To audience:*)
Checking in with my wife.
                    (*Into phone:*)
Miss Blondell's room, please.
                    (*After a moment:*)
She doesn't answer?

No message. Thank you.

No, wait!

Tell her her husband called.

Thank you.

                    He hangs up, sits behind
                    desk; lights cigarette.

                    (*To audience:*)
My wife is out. She's probably at rehearsal.

She's starring in a show for Mike Todd.

It's the national company of a musical Ethel Merman did on Broadway.

Todd has taken an interest in her...and vice versa.

Joan just did a show for Todd...and it flopped.

They didn't get along then, but now....
                    (*Ponders, then:*)
You're here because I need to talk, and talking to you is like talking to myself.

It helps me see things more clearly.

I should do it more often, but I don't have the time.

When I'm not doing a film, I have business interests.

Real estate: There's only so much of it.
                    (*Ponders, then:*)
When I came to Hollywood in 1931, I planned to stay until I made $100,000. Then, I was going to leave.

But, it didn't work out that way.

I found I wasn't just working for money.

To know and to do became important.
                    (*Stands; paces.*)
Don't get the wrong idea.

Money-wise, I did okay before Hollywood.

I made a thousand dollars a week at the Stanley Theatre in Pittsburgh.

I sang. I was the emcee...orchestra leader....

I was "Richard E. Powell, concert tenor".

But, as young and inexperienced as I was then, I saw the handwriting on the wall.

The movies loomed like nice fresh territory to an explorer...even if my weekly salary got cut to three hundred dollars a week.

I know. You don't have to say it.

I'm supposed to be a shrewd businessman, but sometimes you have to gamble.

Four years earlier, I didn't gamble.

A Fox talent scout saw me; wanted to sign me for the lead in *Seventh Heaven*.

I didn't want to leave Pittsburgh, so they hired Charles Farrell.

At the Oscars...the very first Oscars...*Seventh Heaven* was nominated for Best Picture; Janet Gaynor won Best Actress and Frank Borzage won for Director.

I was a singer. What was I going to sing in a silent movie?

I'm getting ahead of myself, aren't I?

Why am I asking you that?

You don't know where I'm going with this.

I'm not even sure if I know where I'm going with this.

So, just listen.

I'm at a crossroads....

In my career....

My marriage....

I need that role in *Double Indemnity*.

I'm too old to be the "boy singer" any more.

I know they're one of the biggest box-office draws in the business, but playing second-fiddle in an Abbott and Costello movie was not a smart career move.
(Shrugs)
Thirty grand is thirty grand.

Where do you think I get the money to invest in real estate?

I started in life with two assets: a voice that didn't drive audiences onto the streets, and the determination to make money.

I've always worked like a dog. If you don't keep working hard in this business, you're dead.

I guess it all began when I was a kid in Little Rock, Arkansas.

I was a boy soprano, and then a tenor.

Other kids with good voices sang in their church choirs.

I did, too -- every Sunday morning at the Episcopal church where my family were parishioners.

But, just to cover myself, I also sang in the Presbyterian church on Sunday night...at the Masonic Lodge on Wednesday night...and at the Jewish synagogue on Friday night.

I was so busy, I could have used MCA to represent me in those days.

But, it paid off.

The local railroad station master paid me five cents a chorus to hear "Casey Jones".
                    (Sings:)
"Casey Jones--mounted to his cabin,
"Casey Jones--with his orders in his hand,
"Casey Jones--mounted to his cabin,
"And he took his farewell trip to that promis'd land."
                    (Speaks:)
Okay, I've sung for you.

But, that song is in the public domain, so there's no royalty to be paid.

Where were we?

After I got out of high school and finished two years at Little Rock College -- working my way through as a soda jerker, a telephone company order-taker, and a grocery clerk -- a non-Episcopal source recommended me to an outfit called the Royal Peacock Orchestra in Louisville, Kentucky, and I got my start in show business...which I always wanted.

On stage, I sang "The Kashmiri Song" in a high-whining voice.

The Royal Peacock Orchestra ran out of money in a mining town: Herrin, Illinois.

I'd never heard of the place either.

To make matters worse, there was a murder near the dance hall where we were playing, which resulted in the orchestra being blacklisted...even though we were all innocent.

I figured the trend toward high-whining semi-classical tenors was over, so I learned to play the banjo.

My mother played the piano. She gave lessons to me and my brother, Howard.

Howard was so much better than me that I got disgusted and quit, and started studying the clarinet, trumpet, and saxophone....

And now, the banjo.

Got a job singing with Charlie Davis and his orchestra.

———

That led to me becoming the permanent master-of-ceremonies at theaters in Indianapolis....where I introduced a then-unknown actress named Ginger Rogers.

Ginger's mother didn't like the way I introduced her daughter.

She came backstage and chewed my ear off.

Sure you won't have some coffee?
        (Pours himself some coffee.)
Like I said before: I saw it coming.

That's what makes you a success in this business...any business.

You anticipate.

Before talking pictures, every big movie house had stage shows booked out of New York.

For about three years, the movie theater emcee was the kingpin of the industry. The Brooklyn Paramount had Rudy Vallee...the Stanley Theater in Jersey City had Stubby Kaye...and so on.

We did everything -- told jokes, led the band, introduced the acts, played skits with the touring movie stars.

The people got to know us, and week after week, they'd come to see us, even more than the visiting celebrities on the bill. It was great experience.

I remember one time in Pittsburgh, Jean Harlow came through.

She said "Thank you," and walked off the stage before I could lift my baton to lead the orchestra.

I took her aside and said, "Look, honey, you've got to have an act."

I taught her corny jokes -- like I said, "I bet you a dime I can kiss you without touching you."

I kissed her, and she said, "You touched me."

I then gave her a dime and said, "You're right. But, it was worth it."

She used that bit for years after that.

PHONE RINGS.

Powell shrugs; crosses to phone.

(*To audience:*)
When it stops ringing, that's when I'll start worrying.
(*Into phone:*)
Hello.

Oh, hello, June.
(*To audience:*)
A young actress I worked with: June Allyson.
(*Into phone:*)
Yes, we're meeting at eight at my house.

You know the address. You've been here before.

No, Joan doesn't mind. She's in New York;
rehearsing a play.

See you then.
                    (*Hangs up; to audience:*)
I did a picture with Lucille Ball at Metro a couple
years ago, *Meet the People*, and June was in the cast.

I have her and other young actors and actresses up to
the house every now and then; give them advice on
how to survive in this business..

We talk about scripts...judging roles...working with
the studio....

They've got to learn that you're only as welcome in
this town as your last picture.

It will be interesting to see who's still among us ten
years from now, and who's back home working in the
shoe store.

June?

I first met her when she was in *Best Foot Forward* on
Broadway.

This little "midget" came on stage, opened her mouth
to sing, and out boomed a husky voice like Jimmy
Durante's...but froggier.

She was terrific.

Joan and I went backstage and congratulated her.

———

Actually, I congratulated her. Joan just stood there.

I'd forgotten all about that until June reminded me at MGM.

Poor kid.

Her father was an alcoholic; abandoned his family when she was six months old.
                    (*Ponders:*)
Later....

They were going to test her for a picture with Durante and Van Johnson: *Two Girls and a Sailor.*

She called me at home.

Joan didn't like that. In fact, we were in the middle of an argument when she called.

We always seem to be arguing these days.

Anyway, June wanted advice on the script.

I read it; took her to lunch at the Brown Derby.

I suggested that she switch roles with Gloria DeHaven, her co-star, and play the plain sister while DeHaven play the glamorous one.

That girl has guts.

She was terrified, but she went up to Louis B. Mayer's office and told him she wanted to play the plain sister...and that's what happened.

I don't think Gloria DeHaven has ever forgiven me for that.

(*Lights cigarette.*)

Did I tell you I was married?

I mean, before Joan.

It didn't last very long.

Her name was Mildred Maund.

She used to come visit our neighbors back in Little Rock, and I thought marriage would be proof of my manhood.

Mildred wasn't interested in show business.

I traveled, and she stayed at home. It wasn't fair.

She realized as well as I did that I was not about to turn back from this line of work.

We barely lasted two years.

But, we ended on a friendly basis....

As well as any marriage can end on a friendly basis.

Enough of that sidebar. Let's get back to the main story.

One of Jack Warner's nephews spotted me on stage and, to cut a long story short, I was cast in a film, called *Blessed Event*.

I was going to be in a movie!

Instead of staying home the night before we started shooting and worrying about it, I went to a Hollywood nightclub and stayed out 'till three in the morning.

Not too smart.

I sang three bad songs in *Blessed Event*, one of which was a commercial for a shoe store which Louise Fazenda -- Hal Wallis' wife -- ran in the picture.

I had one word of dialog, "Hiya," which I said to Lee Tracy.

I don't know why, but *Blessed Event* was a hit, and I was a hit.

The next thing I knew, I was signed to a long-term Warner Brothers contract.

I went to Hollywood and did one picture after another in which I sang songs -- usually in a soldier, sailor or marine suit -- and said not much more than "Hiya".

I know. *42nd Street, Footlight Parade* and the *Gold Diggers* movies were all big hits, but that's because of Busby Berkeley, not me.

Who can ever forget the "Lullaby of Broadway" number from *Gold Diggers of 1935*?

It's a miracle nobody was killed doing his musical numbers.

(Sings)
"There's Busby Berkeley.
How high the boom."
(Speaks:)
We used to sing that behind his back.

Actually, Buzz was a genius...a madman....

He could do anything.

And, all I had to do, day in and day out, was say "Hiya," "I love you, honey," and sing a song to Ruby Keeler.

I was so insipid in those pictures, I wanted to throw up.

I liked Ruby, and I was a big fan of her husband, Al Jolson.

He was the world's greatest entertainer.

All you had to do was ask him. He'd tell you.

Sometimes you didn't even have to ask.

When I got the script for *Wonder Bar*, I was very excited that I was finally going to work with him.

That changed when we went into production.

Jolson went to Lloyd Bacon, the director; tried to take the good song that was assigned to me, and leave me with the eight bars he didn't like.

Lloyd didn't go for it .

Neither did Jack Warner.

So, I kept my songs, and Jolson got to go to heaven on a mule.

If you see the picture, you'll know what I'm talking about.

I wasn't surprised when Ruby divorced Jolson.

I just wonder what took her so long.

I got cast in two movies with Marion Davies.

We did the one film together, then she requested me for the second.

She liked me.

Too much.

I liked her, too, but except for some late night phone calls, I kept my distance.

You think I wanted to make an enemy of William Randolph Hearst?

Remember what happened to Thomas Ince?

You think I wanted to get shot?

Every so often, I'd complain to Jack Warner:

"Can't you please cast me in something other than a musical?

"I'm not a kid anymore, but I'm still playing boy scouts."

Once he said: "You want to do a movie with Jimmy Cagney?"

"Not another *Footlight Parade*?"
                    (*As Warner:*)
"No. Nothing like that."

"Then, yes," I said. "Absolutely!"

I figured I was going to do a gangster picture; a real shoot 'em up.

The movie was *A Midsummer Night's Dream.*

Shakespeare.

I played "Lysander".
                    (*Recites:*)
"The course of true love never did run smooth."

I was terrible.

Cagney was lucky.

He played "Bottom," and half the movie he got to wear a donkey's head.

They cast me in more musicals.

I went back to Warner. Said: "If you don't have something better for me, loan me out to another studio.

They lent me to Fox.

What did they cast me in?

A musical.
                    (*Ponders, then:*)
After years of doing one musical after another at Warner Brothers, I had learned two things.

I knew I wasn't the greatest singer in the world, and I saw no reason why an actor should restrict himself to one particular phase of the business.

My contract was almost up, so I went to Warner and rebelled.

I wanted to do some of the roles that Cagney...Paul Muni...and Edward G. Robinson were doing...but not Shakespeare.

He offered me more money.

I said, "No!".

It wasn't about the money.

I was always cast in the same stupid story, and I never had anything sensible to say.

Jack turned me down, and I've never worked at Warner Brothers since.

You might say, that's when I found sanity.

PHONE RINGS.

*Powell shrugs to audience; crosses
to desk; sits as he answers it.*

Hello.
                    (*To audience:*)
My agent.
                    (*Into phone:*)
So, what did Wilder say?

He cast who!?!

Fred MacMurray!?!

I know he's done dramatic films before.

I can play drama.

It Happened Tomorrow, the United Artists picture I
did for Rene' Clair....

That was a drama...sort of.

What are they offering?

Bring on the Girls?

With Veronica Lake and Spike Jones.

A musical.

I pass.

I don't care if they suspend me. This is the end of
the road for me.

Hangs up phone.

(To himself:)
Double Indemnity: That should have been my part.

Stands; paces.

(To audience:)
I signed with Paramount because I thought they
would cast me in something other than musicals.

They did...once.

And, in all fairness, Preston Sturges' *Christmas in
July* is a marvelous little classic.

Some people think it's my best performance.

But, it was the same kind of light role I was doing
before...without the singing.

After that, I'm working with Mary Martin, Betty
Hutton and Abbott and Costello....

Singing.

(Ponders, then:)
Before we leave Warner Brothers, we have to talk
about my wife, Joan Blondell.

We did over a half dozen pictures together at the
studio: *42nd Street...Footlight Parade...Gold
Diggers.....*

She was separated from George Barnes, a cinematographer. He shot *Footlight Parade... Dames....*

He was one of the best in the business. Recently, he's been working for Hitchcock.

They had a son, Norman...

Barnes didn't want children.

The funny thing is, in the movies I made with Joan at Warner Brothers, we were never paired together.

I was with Ruby Keeler and she was with somebody else.

Joan and I started having lunches together, then dinners.

I introduced her to my parents. They approved of her.

We were married on a yacht in San Pedro.

I thought it was the greatest event of my life.

Some of our fans didn't agree.

They were furious that I hadn't married Ruby Keeler.

We honeymooned in New York...and I came down with a bad cold.
                    (*Chuckles.*)
While I was coughing and sneezing in bed, Joan finished reading *Gone With the Wind*.

Selznick offered her the role of "Belle Watling" in the movie version, but she turned it down.

I don't blame her.

Belle was the local madam, and once the censors got through with it, there wasn't much left to the part.
(Ponders:)
Eight years later....
(To audience:)
I adopted Joan's son, Norman.

He's "Norman Powell" now.

We also have a daughter, Ellen.

And now, Joan's back in New York with Mike Todd, and I'm on suspension from Paramount.

He picks up the copy of Variety *from his desk; glances at an article.*

(To himself:)
That looks interesting.

When one door closes, another opens.
(To audience:)
Excuse me a minute.

I'm calling my agent.
(Picks up phone; dials:)
This is Dick Powell. Is he in?
(After a moment:)
No, I haven't changed my mind.

30

What do you mean: "It's too late anyway."?

Really? Who did they cast in....

What was it called? *Bring on the Girls*?

Sonny Tufts!?!

Good for them.

I know I'm still on suspension, but that's not why I called.

They're going to shoot a Raymond Chandler movie over at RKO.

I want to play Philip Marlowe.

Farewell, My Lovely...but they'll probably change the title.

I know Chandler was one of the writers on *Double Indemnity*, but he didn't nix me for the part.

Writers don't have that kind of power.

Call RKO and tell them, if they let me play Philip Marlowe, I'll do a musical for them.

Two musicals.

My Paramount contract?

Let me worry about that.

If worse comes to worse, I'll go to Frank Freeman, get down on my hands and knees and beg him to release me.

If I won't do any more of his musicals, why would he want to keep me?

Yes, I'm sure.

Okay. Call me back.

Hangs up; paces.

(*To audience:*)
I've read *Farewell, My Lovely.*

It's about a tough, cynical, hard-boiled private eye.

It's the same genre as *The Maltese Falcon*...and you know what that picture did for Humphrey Bogart.
(*Lights cigarette.*)
What were we talking about?

That's right: Joan.

We do have our issues.

Doesn't every couple?

In our case....

These days, it seems to be about everything.
(*Indicates surroundings.*)
Take our house here.

Beautiful, isn't it?

We have a pool...tennis court....

The difference between Joan and me is that, she looks at this as a "home".

For me, it's an investment.

I can't tell you how upset she was when I sold our house on Maple.

Maybe I should have asked her first before I did it, but still....

I know she loved that house....

But, we made a hell of a profit on the sale....

And, we bought this one: an even better house.

At least, I think so.

Joan just doesn't understand business.

I don't think most women do.

Women want to be romanced.

Romancing takes time.

Time is money.

Don't get me wrong.

We make love.

How else to you think we got our daughter?

Friday nights, I give her "the look".

She gives me "the look".

Then, I go into the bathroom....

I shave.

I shower.

I clip my nails.

Put on my pajamas....

And, I'm ready for romance...right on schedule.

What's wrong with that?

Joan, my wife with the wisecracks, would always
make a remark.
> (*Mimics Joan Blondell:*)
"Good thing we're not Jewish.

"We'd have to do it on Saturday."
> (*Sits; ponders, then:*)
I got Joan to leave Warner Brothers.

It was time.

Cagney had left....

Muni was gone....

I was out of there....

They were giving Joan the Carole Lombard rejects.

She left Warner Brothers; landed right on her feet.

Universal hired her to do a movie with Bing Crosby.

We even did a couple of pictures together.

Model Wife, and....

I Want a Divorce.

Hmmm!
                    (*Ponders.*)
We tried separate vacations.

Joan went to New York. I went fishing.

We came back.

She did another picture.

I looked after the kids...handled our investments
...puttered around in the garage....

We were out on my boat when we heard the Japanese
had bombed Pearl Harbor.

We hurried back into port...raced home....

Put blackout curtains over all our windows....

We did USO shows at the military bases...the Hollywood Canteen....

I was in *Star Spangled Rhythm*, Paramount's all-star military flag waver.

At MGM, Joan played a nurse on Bataan in *Cry Havoc*.

And, now, she's in New York with Mike Todd.

Forget vacations: We really lead separate lives these days.
            (*Ponders, then:*)
Things are becoming clearer now.

Thank you.

                              PHONE RINGS.

                    Powell crosses to answer it.

Hello?
            (*To audience:*)
My agent.
            (*Into phone:*)
So, what did RKO have to say?

They're changing the title of the picture to *Murder, My Sweet*.

Okay, but what about me?

Good news and bad news.

36

Give me the bad first.

Eddie Dmytryk is against it.

So is Adrian Scott.

They can't see me as Philip Marlowe.

Well, they're just the director and the producer. What do they know?

So, what's the good news?

The studio likes the idea....

...of my doing two musicals for them.

And, they're willing to pay that price....

...providing *my* price is right.
                    (*Ponders, then to audience:*)
Sometimes you have to gamble.
                    (*Into phone:*)
They're not planning to turn *Murder, My Sweet* into a musical, are they?

Thank God for that.

Make the best deal you can.

I know you will.

He hangs up.

(*Paces, then:*)
Now, I just have to get out of my Paramount contract.
(*Muses:*)
Philip Marlowe: tough, cynical, hard-boiled private
eye....

> *He looks into the mirror; tries
> out some tough, cynical, hard-
> boiled private eye expressions.*

> PHONE RINGS.

They couldn't have made a deal that quickly.

> *He answers the phone.*

Hello?

Yes, I'll accept a collect call from Mrs. Powell.
(*To audience:*)
Joan.
(*Into phone:*)
Hello, dear. How are you?

Everything's under control here. The kids are fine.

I may be doing a picture at RKO.

No, not a musical.

How's the play going?

Ethel Merman's being catty?

She sits in the front row at rehearsals, and that bugs
you?

That's Ethel for you.

After all, she did originate the part, and now you're taking it on the road.

Maybe she's afraid of the competition.

I'm not defending her.

Why did you call?

That's right. I called you.

We need to talk.

> *He covers the phone mouthpiece*
> *with his hand; whispers to audience,*
> *as he gestures them to leave.*

This is private. We'll talk again later.
                    (*Into phone.*)
How's Mike Todd?

I'm asking because I hear things.

There's been a couple of blind items in the papers.

LIGHTS BEGIN TO FADE.

I don't know. That's why I'm asking you.

We can talk on the phone....

Or, I can get on a plane, fly back there and we can have this conversation in person.

What's your pleasure?

BLACKOUT.

END OF ACT ONE

ACT II

AT RISE: *The stage is empty.*
O.S. We hear DICK POWELL,
singing "Over There".

POWELL *(O.S.)*
(Sings)

"Over there, over there
"Send the word, send the word over there."

> *Powell enters. He's 12 years older;*
> *dressed in a different sport coat*
> *and slacks; white shirt, but still no tie.*

> *He acknowledges the audience;*
> *continues to sing.*

"That the Yanks are coming
"The Yanks are coming
"The drums rum-tumming
"Everywhere."

(Speaks to audience:)
I love this song.

I used to sing it on Armed Forces Radio during the war.

(Sings:)
"So prepare, say a prayer.
"Send the word, send the word to beware.

41

"We'll be over, we're coming over
"And we won't come back till it's over
"Over there."

> *Sits behind desk; puts his feet up.*

> *(Speaks to audience:)*
It's been a few years, hasn't it?

How have you been?

When did we last talk?

It was about the time I did *Murder, My Sweet*, wasn't it?

Wow! A lot has happened since then.

Obviously, I've got some issues to talk to you about.

Otherwise, you wouldn't be here, would you?

> *Stands; paces.*

I guess the first thing I should do is bring you up to date.

I did *Murder, My Sweet*.

Claire Trevor was in it. So was Mike Mazurki.

You know Mike. He's gentle as a lamb, but he always plays thugs.

Mike was supposed to tower over me in that film, but I'm 6'2" and he's only an inch or two taller.

In our scenes together, I had to stand in a trench.

There was some great dialogue in that picture.
(*As Philip Marlowe:*)
"'Okay Marlowe,' I said to myself. 'You're a tough guy. You've been sapped twice, choked, beaten silly with a gun, shot in the arm until you're crazy as a couple of waltzing mice.

"'Now let's see you do something really tough - like putting your pants on.'"
(*To audience:*)
That's a lot better line than "Hiya," isn't it?

Murder, My Sweet was a hit.

It was such a hit that RKO told me to forget the musicals I'd agreed to do for them. They wanted me to do more "tough guy" roles.

And, that's what I did for the next few years....

Film Noir, they call it:

Bogart's *The Maltese Falcon* may have been the first "official" *Film Noir* to come out of Hollywood, but *Murder, My Sweet* started the trend.

Cornered...Johnny O'Clock...Cry Danger....

I also did films that were not *Noir*.

___
43

Station West was a Western....

Rogues Regiment had me in the French Foreign Legion....

I played a Mountie in *Mrs. Mike*.

The Tall Target: That was an interesting one.

It was, supposedly, based on a true story.

I was a former police detective who foils a plot to assassinate Abe Lincoln *before* his inauguration.
                    (*Smiles.*)
So, where was he that night at Ford's Theater?

The best part?

I didn't have to sing in any of those pictures.

                              He lights a cigarette.

If you read the newspapers, you know that Joan and I divorced...not long after I saw you last.

She married Mike Todd...and that lasted about three years.

I married June Allyson.

The wedding was like any other wedding...except for the fact that the bride was positive I wouldn't show up.

I can't think of why.

What guy would welsh on marrying a girl like June?

Maybe I fell in love with those Peter Pan collars she wears.

Louis B. Mayer walked her down the aisle.

That was after he suspended her for agreeing to marry me in the first place.

Why would he object?

I was twice divorced....

Thirteen years older than her....

And, here we are.

I call her "Monkeyface".
                    (*Shrugs.*)
When I'm irritated with her, I call her "Flattop'.

June and I have two kids.

Pamela is adopted. And, we did one the old fashioned way.

A son: Richard Jr.
                    (*Chuckles to himself
                    to hide a tear, then.*)
She was preparing to do *Royal Wedding* with Fred Astaire.

She called him. Said: "Fred, I'm pregnant!"

Fred's reaction: "Who is this?"
(*Chuckles:*)
They replaced her with Jane Powell.

I stopped acting in movies two years ago.

The last one I did was *Susan Slept Here* with Debbie Reynolds.

You'll note that I said acting in movies.

I produce and direct films now, and any acting I do is strictly on television.

In all my years in films, there there's only one role that I really wanted to do.

Yes, I wanted to play Philip Marlowe, but that was a career move to get me out of musicals.

The part that I would have given my right arm to play was "Captain Queeg" in *The Caine Mutiny*.

Couldn't you see me as that paranoid son-of-a-bitch?

I went to Stanley Kramer at Columbia; begged him for the role.

"Sorry, Dick," he said. "I've already cast Humphrey Bogart.

Then, Paul Gregory offered me the part in *The Caine Mutiny Court Martial*, which was going to do a twenty week national tour before it landed on Broadway.

46

(*Chuckles*)
I would have taken the part, but June said if I was
away for that long, she'd leave me.

So, I wound up directing it, until....

PHONE RINGS.

He crosses to phone; answers it.

Hello?

Of course, I'm in for him.
(*Covers mouthpiece; to audience:*)
Howard Hughes.
(*Into phone:*)
Hello, Howard.

Tonight?

Okay.

He hangs up. Ponders,
then speaks to audience.

He wants to see me at midnight.

And, I'll be there.

One time, he called about three in the morning; woke
us up.

He wanted to come over...right then.

He told me to turn off all the lights in the house.

—

June insisted on meeting him.

I didn't think that was a good idea, but what was I going to do?

Lock her in a closet?

It was her house, too.

I think she was shocked when she saw him.

He was dressed like...Howard Hughes....

Like a bum: tattered sweat shirt...tattered pants...no socks...and tennis shoes that were falling apart.

Then, June committed the cardinal sin.

She grabbed Howard Hughes' hand and shook it.

Nobody touches Howard Hughes.

He's afraid of germs.

I know he's a weird duck, but he does own RKO Pictures....

June said: "If I get a divorce, I'm naming Howard Hughes as co-respondent."
            (*Chuckles, then:*)
This is one of the issues I wanted to talk to you about.

Howard Hughes gave me the opportunity to direct.

———

The picture was called *Split Second*; sort of an updated version of *The Petrified Forest*.

Stephen McNally played an escaped convict, holding a group of people hostage in the Nevada desert...right on the location where they were doing the atomic bomb tests.

It was a pretty good picture. Alexis Smith was in it. So was Jan Sterling.

After that, I looked for other opportunities to direct...which is how I wound up directing *The Caine Mutiny Court Martial*.

Henry Fonda was the star, playing the role that Jose Ferrer did in the film, and Lloyd Nolan was Captain Queeg.

Five days before we opened, Howard called me. Said they needed me immediately back in Hollywood to start filming *Susan Slept Here*.

I assured Paul Gregory that the performances were set, and they really didn't need me any more.

You know what Gregory, that son-of-a-bitch, did?

The minute I left, he hired Charles Laughton to take over as director and, when the play opened, I got no credit whatsoever.

The play was a hit, and now I'm suing Gregory for what I'm entitled to.

(Responds to somebody in the audience:)

What?

No, I'm not Hughes' lap dog.

I want something from him, and I'm willing to put up with his crap until I get it.

What do I want?
(Ponders, then:)
Later.

The best thing about switching from being an actor to being a director is that you don't have to shave or hold your stomach in ay more,

Right now, I'm waiting for *The Conqueror* to be released.

That's the film about Genghis Khan I started directing two years ago.

Don't tell Howard, but I would have directed it for nothing.

Howard likes to futz around with his movies, which is why its taken so long.

The project was written with Marlon Brando in mind for the lead, but John Wayne owed RKO a film as part of a three-picture deal and I was assigned to direct whatever that film might be.

"Duke" and I were in my office, going over various scripts, when I was called away for a few minutes. When I got back, he was reading the script for *The Conqueror*, and he was very excited about it.

I tried to talk him out of it. I'd read the script and didn't like it.

But, he insisted that this was the film he wanted to make.

Who am I to turn down John Wayne?

Even if he wanted to play Genghis Khan.

Hughes gave me carte blanche.

Huge budget.

He wanted me to make the biggest spectacular ever.

We shot *The Conqueror* in Utah, near the spot where they'd done the atomic bomb tests a few years earlier.

Not to worry. The Government assured Howard that the location was perfectly safe..

Howard even had sixty tons of sand shipped from Utah to the studio in Hollywood just to make sure the interior shots matched.

He's very excited about this picture.

We've got a great cast. Aside from Wayne, there's
Susan Hayward, Agnes Moorehead, Pedro
Armendariz....

I think we've got a hit on our hands.

> *Looks about to make sure*
> *he's alone, then whispers:*

If we do, I'm thinking that Howard might ask me to
run RKO for him.
> (*Normal voice:*)

That'd be something, wouldn't it?

A former crooner running a major Hollywood studio.

Or, maybe not.

A couple of years ago, I looked around and saw that
the movie business was going badly. All the studios
had dropped their contract players and it was getting
tougher and tougher to make a buck.

I had been fascinated by the new medium, television,
ever since we began to get network shows in
California.

I figured it was time to break in on the wrestling and
the comedy shows with good Hollywood drama..

I got together with my friends Charles Boyer,
Rosalind Russell and Joel McCrea, and we planned
an anthology series to be called "Four Star
Playhouse".

But, Roz and Joel took one look at themselves in the kinescopes, and they said, "This stuff will never make it. Besides, the work is too hard."

So, they backed out, leaving only me and Boyer.

I finally rounded up David Niven, and I went to New York to try to sell "Four Star Playhouse" with only three stars.

I was lucky.

I ran into a man who was the director of my old radio series, "Richard Diamond, Private Detective".

That's right. I had my own radio series for four years, which I managed to do along with my movie work.

This man, Nat Wolf, was the new head of television programming for a big advertising agency.

He sold our show to the Singer Sewing Machine Company, and we were on our way.

Charles, David and I alternate in a different story every week, along with our fourth star, Ida Lupino.

I'm the president of Four Star Productions, and I don't have anybody over me to answer to.

Not even Howard Hughes.
                    (*Ponders.*)
Not even Howard Hughes.....

PHONE RINGS.

Powell is startled; looks about,
wondering if somebody is listening.
Hesitantly, he approaches
the phone; answers it.

Hello?

Oh, Sue....How are you?
      (*Breathes a sigh of relief; to audience:*)
It's Sue Ladd, Alan's wife.

June and Alan are doing a picture together at Warner
Brothers.
      (*Into phone:*)
What's that, Sue?

Am I aware that Alan is in love with my wife, June?
      (*Chuckles.*)
Isn't everybody?

Calm down. I've read the gossip columns, and that's
all they are: gossip.

No, June and I are fine.

No problems whatsoever.
      (*Slightly hesitant.*)
Of course, we can have dinner together soon.

We can clear this matter up.

Let me check with June. She keeps our social
schedule.

54

By the way, June tells me that Alan would like to play Lawrence of Arabia.

That would be quite a change for him.

Maybe somebody will make a movie about Lawrence one day.

Me?

No, I just finished a desert picture. I got sunburned enough.

Okay, Sue. I'll speak to June.

Hangs up phone.

(*To audience:*)
Did I sound convincing?

I know why Alan wants to play Lawrence of Arabia.

Lawrence was only five-foot-three, and Alan is just two or three inches taller.

They could hire actors to play opposite him who wouldn't have to stand in a trench.

Digging trenches takes time and, in the movie business, time is money.
(*To himself:*)
Now, I'm being catty.
(*To audience:*)
June and I are having our issues these days....

───

That's the other thing I wanted to talk to you about.

She doesn't think I pay enough attention to her.

But, in all fairness....

I've been busy making a living...for both of us.

The Conqueror....

I have my responsibilities to Four Star....

I watch our investments....

And, as you've noticed, when Howard Hughes says "Jump," I jump.

When June and I first got married, it was different.

We did a couple more pictures together: *The Reformer and the Redhead*....

I was the reformer and she was the redhead.

I'd buy a house for us....

Didn't matter if she saw it first. She always said she liked it.

She knew I was older; more experienced in these things, and I knew better.

June would go out and buy furniture.

I'd see what she bought...then send it back and choose something that was more suitable for the house.

She said she was happy with my choices.

She was working all the time anyway.

She did movies with Bogie...Bill Holden...Jimmy Stewart...

(*Chuckles*)

June is such a good wife that Jimmy married her three times.

Producers were always casting her as the nice, understanding wife...who went along.

She's become one of the highest paid actresses in the business...and she has absolutely no idea what she earns.

I handle the money...invest it....

She trusts my instincts completely.

Sometimes she says she's married to a telephone.

June tried to change her "goody two-shoes" image recently.

She did a picture with Jose Ferrer, *The Shrike*. It was adapted from a Pulitzer Prize-winning play.

She'd wanted to play a dramatic, villainous role for a long time, and she practically begged them to give her the part.

I warned her: "I begged Stanley Kramer to let me play 'Captain Queeg,' and look where it got me."

I guess June is a better beggar than me, because they cast her.

A shrike is an innocent-looking bird who likes to impale its victim on a thorn.

In other words, in this film, June would be playing a sweet-looking, but vicious, bitch.

The preview audiences hated the picture.

They said "June Allyson would never, ever put her husband in an insane asylum and leave him there. She'd at least get him out."

They had to reshoot the end of the picture where she went back to the insane asylum, so she could be... good.

The movie still lost money.

The public will never accept June as anything but the good wife and the girl next door.

If you want to be successful in this business, you go where the money is.

That's what I've always tried to do, and our finances prove it.

Where June and I started butting heads was when I sold the house with out telling her.

June is just like Joan was when it comes to houses.

She looks at a house as a home.

I look at it as an investment.

I bought acreage.

We moved to a little farm.

We had chickens...geese...sheep....

One Christmas, I built Ricky his own baseball diamond....

Pammy got a riding ring with jumps to take her horse over....

I don't know why June hated the gift I gave her that year for Christmas: New linoleum for the kitchen.

She never goes in there anyway.

We have a cook.
                    (*Beat*)
What did you expect me to get her?

Diamonds?

She has diamonds.
                    (*Beat*)
June says she wants to stay home; spend more time with the kids.

—

I told her: Once you lose your momentum in this business, it's difficult to get it back.

And now, she's doing *The McConnell Story* with Alan Ladd....

And, I'm kissing Howard Hughes' ass.

The truth is that I don't consider myself to be an overworked man.

I have enough worries that I don't oversleep.

I have enough things to do that I don't have time to overeat.

I've worked hard all my life. I think that's pretty much what life is all about.

I kid around and say I work because, with things the way they are, I'll have to be earning money ten years after I'm in the grave to get my four kids through college.

But, that's not true. I work because it is the only way to keep ahead.

What counts most in this profession is survival.

There were lots of stars bigger than I, but I've seen them come and go.

Somehow, I've managed to survive, and that's what I'm proud of.

(Chuckles)

It's no secret that I'm a lifelong Republican.

One of my closest friends, ever since our days at Warner Brothers together, is Ronnie Reagan.

All his friends call him "Ronnie".

Almost every time we got together, George Murphy, Ronald Colman and I would try to convince Ronnie of the error of his ways...for being a lifelong Democrat.

He definitely has a political mind set.

For years, he was president of Screen Actors' Guild...and an effective one.

Then, he met Nancy Davis, now Nancy Reagan.

Awhile later, I'm lecturing Ronnie about his politics, and all of a sudden he stopped me.

"Hold on," he said. "You don't have to harangue me any more. I've switched. I'm a Republican."

I couldn't believe it.

Did Nancy show him the error of his ways, or did I?

Now, I'm wondering if the son of a bitch is going to run for President some day.
>   (*Chuckles, then mimics:*)
"He's going to win one for the Gipper."
>   (*Ponders*)

I was watching one of my old movies on television last night: *Flirtation Walk* with Ruby Keeler.

I was never that young or that thin.

When we first started "Four Star Playhouse" back in 1952, we signed a well-known actress for one of the first shows.

She reported to work, then spent half the day in her dressing room, combing her hair.

Eventually, she appeared on the set, but I wasn't there.

I was shooting a scene on another part of the soundstage.

She came over to me, said "Okay, I'm ready.".

"I'm sorry, honey" I said, "but this isn't the movies.

"We cancelled you out. While you were combing your hair, we assembled a cast and shot half of another script."

(*Shrugs*)

That's the business of television.

With Four Star, Boyer, Niven and I agreed to defer our salaries in order to make good pictures.

The first year, we lost $140,000.

The second year, we broke even.

I seriously doubt if we do any better this year.

But, we believe that, eventually, films with quality, films of lasting value, will pay off.
(*Chuckles.*)
You know, I love them, but most of my fellow actors are idiots.

They get suckered into deals because promoters play on their vanity, and because they are promised the negatives of the filmed TV shows they do.

They think they're going to become millionaires, but they're as stupid as the hicks who thought they were buying the Brooklyn Bridge.

The promoters give them the negatives all right, but they keep syndication and distribution for themselves, so who the hell is the poor slob of an actor going to sell his negatives to?

There I go with another lecture.

Sorry, but I like deals where nobody loses and everybody wins.

Did I tell you that I'm going to play Philip Marlowe again?

If you don't count the appearance I did on Kate Smith's show, it will be my live television debut.

We're doing an hour-long adaptation of Raymond Chandler's *The Long Goodbye* on "Climax".

Teresa Wright and Cesar Romero are also in it.

If it weren't for the fact that I'm playing Philip Marlowe again, the fact that I'm doing live TV would give me opening night butterflies.

But, Marlowe by now is second nature to me. I can ad lib him.

Ad libbing life is not as easy.

Is heading RKO Pictures really worth having to kiss Howard Hughes' ass?

I don't think so.

Four Star may not be into profit yet, but it's on its way.

He crosses to phone; dials:

(*Into phone:*)
Mr. Hughes, please.

Dick Powell.

Please tell him I called, and that I will not be able to make our meeting tonight.

I'd be glad to get together with him during regular business hours.

Yes, I'm sure.

Goodbye.

(Hangs up; speaks to audience:)

See how talking to you makes everything so clear?

My work on *The Conqueror* is finished.

What's he going to do? Burn the negative.
            (Ponders the thought.)
No, he's not that crazy.

He's a businessman.

Of course, he did that other picture with John Wayne,
Jet Pilot, back in 1950...and he still hasn't released
that one.

He's still tinkering with it.

God willing, he won't start tinkering again with *The
Conqueror*.
            (Paces, then to himself:)
You've made your decision, Richard. Live with it!

One down. One to go.

            Picks up phone; dials:

            (Into phone:)
The McConnell Story set, please.

June Allyson, please.

She's rehearsing a scene?

Do you know what time she finishes today?

In about two hours?

This is Dick Powell, her husband.

Would you please tell her to meet me across the street at The Smoke House for dinner?

Thank you. I appreciate it.

He hangs up.

(To audience:)

It's a start.

We'll have a nice dinner.....

We'll come home....

We'll....

You know the rest.

She finishes the picture this week.

Maybe we'll go out on the boat....

Take the kids sailing...down to Mexico.

No, that doesn't work.

I've got to be in New York next week.

Meetings with the network.

Well, tonight'll be a start.

After that, we'll ad lib.
> *(As he heads for the door.)*

Nice chatting with you.

Let's do it again some time.

> *Sings "Pretty Baby".*

"Everybody loves a baby
"That's why I'm in love with you
"Pretty baby, pretty baby...."
> *(Speaks to himself:)*

I can't believe I'm singing a Jolson song.

> *Sings, as he exits.*

"Oh, I want a lovin', baby
"And it might as well be you
"Pretty baby of mine.
"Pretty baby of mine."

> *He is out the door and gone.*

As LIGHTS SLOWLY FADE:

ANNOUNCER
June Allyson filed for divorce, but the couple soon reconciled.

Powell continued to successfully produce and direct for both motion pictures and television until his death at age 58 in 1963.

—

67

A heavy smoker, he died of lung cancer.

However, also victims of cancer were John Wayne, Susan Hayward, Agnes Moorehead, Pedro Armendáriz and approximately one third of the cast and crew who worked on *The Conqueror*, which some have called a "An RKO Radioactive Picture". The film had a respectable box office performance, but was a critical flop.

THE END

THE HOLLYWOOD LEGENDS is a series of one-person, two-act plays by Hollywood biographer, historian, screenwriter and playwright Michael B. Druxman that explore the life and times of some of filmdom's most glittering personalities.

From Clara Bow, "The 'It' Girl" of the silent era, through the birth of the talkies with Al Jolson and Maurice Chevalier, on through the thirties and forties with superstars like Clark Gable, Spencer Tracy, Carole Lombard, Errol Flynn, Basil Rathbone, Ida Lupino, Yvonne De Carlo, Jeanette MacDonald and Nelson Eddy, and, finally, Hollywood's "boy genius," Orson Welles, these anecdote-filled dramatic pieces present a humorous, often touching portrait of each star and the era in which he/she lived.

The collection has now been expanded to include multiple character plays like *LANA & JOHNNY WERE LOVERS*, *SEXY REXY* (Rex Harrison), *B MOVIE*, which deals with the Franchot Tone/ Barbara Payton/Tom Neal scandal of the 1950s, *ROBINSON & RAFT*, *THE LAST MONSTERS*, *AVA & HER GUYS* and BRODERICK CRAWFORD, in which the Oscar-winning actor is "haunted" by the memory of his parents..

The plays, many of which have seen several productions, utilize simple costumes and props, and are designed to be staged on a single setting, with shifts in lighting to denote changes in time and place.

All questions with regard to licensing should be addressed to the author: Michael B. Druxman, PMB 119, 4301 W. William Cannon Dr., Suite B-150, Austin, TX 78749 [*druxy@ix.netcom.com*].

Made in the USA
Middletown, DE
02 June 2021

40867420R00040